T0355924

THIS IS THE STORY OF

THE CHILD RULED BY FEAR

THIS IS THE STORY OF THE CHILD RULED BY FEAR

DAVID GAGNON WALKER

PLAYWRIGHTS CANADA PRESS
TORONTO

This Is the Story of the Child Ruled by Fear © 2024 by David Gagnon Walker
First edition: November 2024
Printed and bound in Canada by Imprimerie Gauvin Ltée, Gatineau

Jacket photo by Henry Chan
Jacket design by Tim Singleton
Author photo by Tori Morrison

Playwrights Canada Press
202-269 Richmond St. W., Toronto, ON M5V 1X1
416.703.0013 | info@playwrightscanada.com | www.playwrightscanada.com

LIBRARY AND ARCHIVES CANADA CATALOGUING IN PUBLICATION
Title: This is the story of the child ruled by fear / David Gagnon Walker.
Names: Walker, David Gagnon, author.
Description: First edition.
Identifiers: Canadiana (print) 20240448804 | Canadiana (ebook) 20240448863
  | ISBN 9780369105271 (softcover) | ISBN 9780369105288 (PDF)
  | ISBN 9780369105295 (EPUB)
Subjects: LCGFT: Drama.
Classification: LCC PS8613.A457 T45 2024 | DDC C812/.6—dc23

Playwrights Canada Press staff work across Turtle Island, on Treaty 7, Treaty 13, and Treaty 20 territories, which are the current and ancestral homes of the Anishinaabe Nations (Ojibwe / Chippewa, Odawa, Potawatomi, Algonquin, Saulteaux, Nipissing, and Mississauga / Michi Saagiig), the Blackfoot Confederacy (Kainai, Piikani, and Siksika), néhiyaw, Sioux, Stoney Nakoda, Tsuut'ina, Wendat, and members of the Haudenosaunee Confederacy (Mohawk, Oneida, Onondaga, Cayuga, Seneca, and Tuscarora), as well as Metis and Inuit peoples. It always was and always will be Indigenous land.

We acknowledge the financial support of the Canada Council for the Arts, the Ontario Arts Council (OAC), Ontario Creates, the Government of Ontario, and the Government of Canada for our publishing activities.

for Tori

FOREWORD

MARCUS YOUSSEF

Shortly before graduating from the National Theatre School of Canada, David Gagnon Walker received the 2018 Playwrights Guild of Canada Emerging Playwright Award. The award included the opportunity to select a mentor, and David chose me. I confess that I was hesitant. Across the country racialized artists like myself were demanding that legacy institutions and art prizes begin to formulate long-overdue responses to questions of race and systemic exclusion. This would be compounded a little over a year later amidst the pandemic and, among other things, the international protests following the murder of George Floyd. I asked myself if I should be putting my limited mentorship energy into a young, white, straightish, cisgender dude "like" David.

The minute we started talking via Zoom, I had my answer. I've been at this work long enough to recognize a certain look in a young artist. A kind of twist in their face, or curl in their lip, or maybe a timbre in their voice. It's something that triggers a feeling in me—that I can see or sense their individuality, their idiosyncrasy, what makes them unique. In part it's vulnerability, I think. And a willingness to not only reveal that vulnerability (or helpful inability to hide it), but also to occupy that vulnerability and move from it with confidence. One look at David through the ether of the Internet and I thought, "Oh, this is going to work. Because I can *see* him."

As is often the case with emerging artists, much of our six-month-long mentorship was spent talking through what it meant to be a recent theatre-school graduate and the various ways he might maximize his odds of being able to make enough money to pay his rent while still writing and making the theatre and live art he is weirdly, idiosyncratically interested in.

Along the way David casually mentioned that he wanted to mine his own experience and write a show about a child overwhelmed by fear. He was starting to develop the kernel of the show in residency with creator/director Christian Barry and Halifax's renowned 2b theatre. David was also sure he wanted the audience to be involved in the storytelling—that it not just be a show, but also a collectively enacted ritual or event. It was early days, so all I did was mention a few examples of artists who have worked with participatory storytelling, most of which he already knew, and encouraged him as best I could, saying, "Yes. That's your impulse. Go for it."

Three years later, as the pandemic ground on through its late stages, I walked into KW Studios in downtown Vancouver to see Pi Theatre's presentation of the national touring production of the play you hold in your hands. To trust your impulse enough to make your first play actually happen shortly after graduating is a gargantuan task. Very few accomplish it. To then turn that production into an eight-city national tour . . . well, it's almost unheard of it. After I saw—or rather participated in—the remarkable play and ritual of collective storytelling, all I could think was, "Thank God he did."

This Is the Story of the Child Ruled by Fear is a sometimes playful, sometimes devastatingly emotional fable. It is also an act of participatory storytelling, and an extraordinary act of grace—even secular communion. It offers its audiences—and now readers—a window into the possibility of collective redemption through faith in the strength of our own fear and vulnerability. Not just showing or sharing that vulnerability but also, as I sensed David doing in our first meeting, confidently occupying it and moving through and from it. In the case of the show, however, we don't just do it alone. We in the audience do it together.

I am a Gen-Xer. Irony is the rhetorical air I breathe, and I'm generationally allergic to what sometimes feels to my fiftysomething self like younger people's fetishization of weakness or victimization as a kind of political badge of honour. Not only that, live performance that asks the audience to participate in its enactment is notoriously difficult to pull off. What could possibly motivate a bunch of strangers with little to no prior connection to the writer/performer and each other to cold read words off a page out loud for sixty minutes, especially when those words ask us to consider the grinding, quiet desperation—David also calls it his depression—lurking at the centre of what we clinically refer to as consciousness, or the feeling of being alive?

Just before David enters the space with a bucket over his head, projected on a screen are these words:

> For this idea to work, seven of you need to take a leap of faith.
> There are seven tables, seven lamps, and seven scripts.
> Each table needs a person at it who is willing to read some lines out loud.
> It's fun, and it's easy. I promise.

Then the projection shifts:

> It's okay if you feel nervous.
> I feel nervous too.
> This is the story of the Child Ruled by Fear.

With this early gesture David begins by acknowledging our fear as people being asked to take a risk and read something we don't know in a roomful of strangers. He acknowledges his own fear of failure. We then participate in the enactment of a fable about the paralytic power of fear. In a stroke of writerly and performative genius that hearkens to the brilliant participatory work of artists like the UK's Duncan Macmillan (*Every Brilliant Thing*) and Brooklyn's 600 Highwaymen (*The Fever, A Thousand Ways*), form and content tell the exact same story. We in the audience are not only told the story of a fictional child, we also engage in that archetypal child's experience, for real and in real time, as we feel our own extreme-stakes fear of performing text out loud in front of strangers. In my experience, seamless, evocative marriage of form and content like this doesn't happen often. When it does, it's often magic. Which is what I believe I and twenty-five or thirty strangers experienced on a rainy, late-pandemic June night in a bunker-like basement theatre in Canada's poorest postal code, Vancouver's Downtown Eastside.

Yes, magic. The magic of a simple, beautifully crafted, impeccably honest, and ferociously unsentimental story about a deep, vibrating secret I go to Herculean efforts to hide every single day of my life. That if I check in at any moment with how I am actually feeling, the answer is often, maybe usually: almost paralyzed by overwhelming, irrational-seeming fear.

In this play, I received concrete and momentarily cathartic evidence that this isn't just me. That I am not alone.

Because it's all of us. Honestly, in these times, how could it not be? (David—holy shit. Congrats!)

Marcus Youssef's fifteen or so plays have been produced in multiple languages in twenty countries across North America, Europe, and Asia, from Seattle to New York to Reykjavik, London, Venice, Hong Kong, Vienna, Athens, Frankfurt, and Berlin. He is the recipient of Canada's largest theatre award, the Siminovitch Prize in Theatre for his body of work as a playwright, as well as Germany's Ikarus Prize, the Vancouver Mayor's Arts Award, the Rio Tinto Alcan Performing Arts Award, the Chalmers Canadian Play Award, the Seattle Times *Footlight Award, the Vancouver Critics Circle Innovation Award (three times), the Victor Martyn Lynch-Staunton Award, and an Honorary Fellowship from Douglas College. Marcus was artistic director of Neworld Theatre in Vancouver from 2005–2019 and co-founded the East Vancouver artist-run production studio Progress Lab 1422. He teaches regularly at the National Theatre School of Canada, UBC, and Studio 58.*

PLAYWRIGHT'S NOTE

Theatre confuses the hell out of me. I believe in it, and I'm disappointed by it. I'm obsessed with it, and I'm exhausted by it. It has given me most of my friendships, and I often have a hard time feeling at home in it. Plays have made me feel very seen and very alone. I think they're amazing, and I think they're kind of dumb.

The book you're holding was born of these contradictions. It's about worry and wonder, loneliness and community, beauty and despair, stories and life. It's me trying to reconcile the things that frustrate me about the art form I've built my world around, and to highlight the things about it I know I love.

What I know for sure is I love rehearsal halls. The process of making plays and performances has enriched my life. By skill set and temperament I'm a writer (which is to say I need lots of time alone with my weird thoughts), and the social aspect of theatre is challenging for me. But collaboration has also changed me in ways I wouldn't trade for anything. It has opened me up to experiences and relationships I would never have imagined for myself when I was a teenager scribbling in a notebook. I don't know if I'm a better person or a better artist than I would have been if I hadn't started spending so much time in collaborative processes, but I'm certainly different: less arrogant, more curious, less methodical, more trusting of myself and the people around me and the indescribable force of creativity that governs the way we live and the things we do.

There is something magical about the first reading of a new play. All the mystery and intensity of the theatre process feel concentrated on the first day of rehearsal, when a group of friends and strangers sit around a table and discover a story together by reading it out loud. Plays never feel more surprising or more alive. For years I talked to anyone who would listen about how I wished productions felt more like readings, and I wondered if there was a way to make some kind of show that would allow audiences to experience the joyful energy that is usually reserved for artists in private rehearsal rooms. I started experimenting with handing audiences scripts and asking them to read things with me.

Eventually I got really literal. What if the show was a table read performed by the audience? I realized this idea would probably be scary to some people. "Audience participation" is a tough ask—everyone seems to have had at least one bad experience with it at some point in their lives—and reading out loud can be pretty anxiety-inducing. So, I figured, if the form is going to be anxiety-inducing, the show should probably be about anxiety.

I had separately been writing strange little stories about a character called the Child Ruled by Fear, who lived in a mythical world of gods, monsters, big cities, and natural disasters. I wasn't sure what to do with this material, but I kept writing it because I enjoyed it, and because it turned into an important outlet. I remember the exact moment I realized these two ideas were in fact one idea. I was sitting at my desk in my new apartment in the North End of Halifax, looking out the window at the flower garden kept by the nice old lady next door, wondering what to make during the residency I had recently started with 2b theatre company. It was suddenly very clear what I wanted to do. From there, things happened pretty fast.

As of this publication, we've done this show in eight venues across Canada, with more presentations on the way. I still get really nervous every time. I know some of our audience volunteers do too. I'm trying to make friends with the feeling. It's sort of what the show is about.

These days it feels like there is much to be afraid of. The climate crisis and the housing crisis and the nobody-agrees-what-reality-is-anymore-thanks-to-the-fucking-Internet crisis can seem like they're squeezing the hope and joy out of every possible future. Being a person is unsolvable, other people are inscrutable, my emotions are unmanageable, my life is unpredictable, and it's easy to feel like I'm the only person alive who feels despondent and confused the way I so often do. And yet I basically believe we all feel that way at least some of the time. If I'm proud of anything about this project, I'm proud of (and honestly a little relieved by) how many people seem to relate to what it explores about my inner life. The Child Ruled by Fear is kind of pathetic. So am I. So are we all. The story the audience and I tell goes to some very silly places and some very dark places, and every performance we go there together, and something passes between us that I can't name but I can see and feel. I'm a person who gets tired of things easily. I don't think I'll ever get tired of performing this show.

I tell the story *with* the audience. That's literally true of this piece, but I also think it's true of all live performance. I've never seen a live work of art that didn't feel to me like it was being created in the moment by everyone present, performers and audience and volunteers and venue staff, all their energies and thoughts and feelings swirling together into this baffling, shimmering thing we call "a show."

This show changed my life. Strange Victory Performance—the producing name Tori Morrison and I chose when we started planning the tour—has become the centre of my career, allowing me to build a company and an artistic practice with my favourite person. I learned things I always wanted to learn and got to do things I always wanted to do thanks to this project and the life it has had.

More intangibly, touring the show has changed my relationship to the art I make and the people I make it for. I don't exactly know what I'm going to do next. I'm sure I'm going to feel just as conflicted and anxious about it as I seem to feel about everything. (Judy Wensel, our co-director, recently gave me a pin to commemorate all my dark nights of the soul; it's on the jacket I wear almost every day.) But I'll be buoyed by this thought: *This Is the Story of the Child Ruled by Fear* is the most I've ever let the conflicted, anxious guy in me control a project, and it is by far the thing I've made that has connected with the most people. I'm starting to think doing this stuff for real means learning to tell the truth. That's scary. Most things worth doing are.

Thank you for reading this book, and for giving this story another kind of life. I hope you enjoy it.

David Gagnon Walker
Toronto, 2024

This Is the Story of the Child Ruled by Fear was created in Halifax during a residency with 2b theatre company, concluding with a public presentation on February 29, 2020, with the following cast and creative team:

Written and performed by David Gagnon Walker
Directed by Christian Barry and Judy Wensel
Sound design, video design, and stage management by Tori Morrison
Lighting design by Christian Barry and Tori Morrison
Scenic design by Morgan Melenka
Technical and design assistance by Lauren Acheson
  and Patricia Vinluan
Dramaturgy by Christian Barry

Since then, the production by Strange Victory Performance has toured Canada, with the following presentations as of November 2024:

The world premiere as part of Common Ground Arts Society's Found Festival at the Studio Theatre, ATB Financial Arts Barn, in Edmonton, AB, from July 8 to 11, 2021.

One Yellow Rabbit's High Performance Rodeo at the Big Secret Theatre, Arts Commons, in Calgary, AB, from May 26 to 28, 2022.

Pi Theatre's Pi Provocateurs Series at KW Studios in Vancouver, BC, from June 2 to 4, 2022.

SummerWorks Performance Festival at the Franco Boni Theatre, the Theatre Centre, in Toronto, ON, from August 4 to 7, 2022.

Theatre Projects Manitoba at Théâtre Cercle Molière, in Winnipeg, MB, from April 28 to 30, 2023.

In the Soil Arts Festival at the Oddfellows Hall in St. Catharines, ON, from June 16 to 18, 2023.

Workshop West Playwrights' Theatre at the Gateway Theatre in Edmonton, AB, from January 31 to February 4, 2024.

This Is the Story of the Child Ruled by Fear continues to tour.

THE SPACE

A circle of tables on stage.
A larger table up stage centre and seven smaller tables.
David sits at the larger table.
The seven smaller tables are seats for audience volunteer readers.
The chairs at these smaller tables all face David.

More audience seats are on risers on three sides in a thrust configuration, or behind the circle in proscenium.
This should feel like standard theatre seating.
David faces the audience.

Each of the seven audience tables has a place card, labelled as such:

THE MINOR GODS

FLOOD

THE TALL FIGURE

THE TALL TALL CHILD

THE MEDIUM TALL CHILD

THE SMALL TALL CHILD

MYSTERIOUS VOICES & THE PUKEY ANTS

Each of the seven audience tables has a copy of the script on it, as well as a reading lamp.
Each script has lines highlighted for the character matching that table's place card.

All named characters in the script are read by the audience members sitting at the tables.
David reads for the narrator.

The whole show is a reading by David and the audience.

There are two live cameras at David's table.
Certain sequences have a live video component.
A large projection screen hangs behind David.

David also has a microphone, only to be used at specific moments, noted in the script.

Tori, the stage manager (among other roles), sits at a technical station visible to the audience. She operates the lights, sound, and video in plain sight.

NARRATION
Text for David is left-justified.

DIALOGUE
Text for the audience is centre-justified.

STAGE DIRECTIONS
Stage directions are right-justified.
Tori reads the scene titles out loud, except for "PROLOGUE."

If we looked inside people, we would find landscapes.
—Agnès Varda, *The Beaches of Agnès*

PROLOGUE

Pre-show music plays.
The audience enters the space.
They've been told by front of house that we need
seven volunteers to sit at the tables on stage.

As they enter, the following text is projected on
the screen, one line at a time, on a loop.
The audience has also received handbills containing
this text on their way into the theatre.

Hello, and welcome.

My name is David.

Right now I have a bucket on my head.

I have an idea to read a play with all of you.

For this idea to work, seven of you need to take a leap of faith.

There are seven tables, seven lamps, and seven scripts.

Each table needs a person at it who is willing
to read some lines out loud.

It's fun, and it's easy. I promise.

It's okay if you feel nervous.

I feel nervous too.

This is the story of the Child Ruled by Fear.

Eventually, seven audience members sit at the
tables, volunteering to read for a character.
The rest of the audience take their seats in the standard theatre seating.

The lights dim, the music fades.

The new lighting state highlights a conspicuous yellow rope on the floor.
It is tied to DAVID's *table and runs across the floor off stage.*

A snowstorm rolls in. Loud sound, video, light.

We hear DAVID's *voice, shouting from off stage:*

Number one!
Number one!

DAVID *enters from where the yellow rope disappears off stage.*
He is holding the rope and using it to guide himself.
He is wearing a bucket on his head.
The bucket has a simple face drawn on it.

He starts guiding himself to his table with the rope.
He continues shouting:

Number one is out of the hut!

This exercise
simulates white-out conditions,
with high winds and blowing snow,
when you can't see your hand in front of your own face.

I can't really tell where I am.
I don't know if you can hear me.
I definitely can't see any of you.

Hello??

Number one is out of the hut!

Aha.
There we are.

> *DAVID finds his seat and sits down at his table.*
> *He takes the bucket off his head.*
> *He looks out at the audience.*

Hi, nice to see you.

My name is David.
I have two email addresses.
They are davidfrederickwalker@gmail.com
and davidgagnonwalker@gmail.com,
which are two versions of my full name.
So now you can email me if you want.

We're in amiskwaciwâskahikan.*
I grew up straddling this continent.
I'm kind of from here in Alberta,
and I'm kind of from Innu territory in Québec.
Right now, we're on Treaty 6 territory,
and I'm grateful to be here today.

I want to tell a story now,
and I'm hoping you'll be kind enough to help.

---

* This paragraph is rewritten in each city where the piece is performed. This version is from the premiere presentation at Common Ground Arts Society's Found Festival.

What we're going to do tonight is a reading.
At certain points we're all going to be invited
to help read this story out loud.

If you're sitting at a table, you probably noticed you
have a lamp and a script in front of you.
Those are your scripts.
You'll each be reading for a character in the story.
You'll know it's time for you to read because the
lamps on your tables will magically turn on.
The pages you'll be reading from are marked with
pink tabs sticking out the side of the binder.
Each of those pages has lines for you which are centre-justified,
and which are highlighted in the same pink colour.

I'll be reading out loud too.
I didn't memorize most of my lines because I'm a lazy man.
I'll be reading for the narrator.
All my lines are left-justified on the page.

So you'll each be reading a character, I'll be reading the narrator.
And there's one special character we all
need to know a bit more about.
He's so special we named the show after him.

> *DAVID holds up the CHILD RULED BY FEAR:*
> *a little animal figurine in a green sweater.*
> *This figure has the same face as the one drawn on DAVID's bucket.*
> *He shows it to the audience, then zooms in on*
> *it with one of the live video cameras.*

This is the Child Ruled by Fear.
What's special about the Child Ruled by Fear is
everyone at a table will take turns reading for him.
Your Child Ruled by Fear pages are marked with blue tabs,
and your Child Ruled by Fear lines are
highlighted in that same blue.

As it happens, one of you should have a blue tab
on the page we're on now.
Could everyone with a script turn to page four?
You'll see, right in the middle of the page, it says DEMONSTRATION.
One of you should have lines highlighted pink, and
one of you should have lines highlighted blue.
They'll be centre-justified on the page.
Found them?
We should have a minor god—raise your hand if that's you—
and the Child Ruled by Fear—there you are.
Great! Okay.
Just to give us all a sense of how these scripts work,
could you two please read this scene
for a minor god and the Child Ruled by Fear?

DEMONSTRATION

A MINOR GOD
Hello
I am a minor god

THE CHILD RULED BY FEAR
Hello, minor god
I am the Child Ruled by Fear

A MINOR GOD
What are you so afraid of, Child Ruled by Fear?

THE CHILD RULED BY FEAR
Lots of things!
Accidents!
Incidents!
Being seen! Being seen! Being seen!

DAVID applauds and encourages the audience to applaud too.

That's all there is to it!

Now, when it comes to the Child Ruled by Fear,
because you'll be taking turns playing him,
there's a vocal quality we like to establish for this character.
I like to imagine that the Child Ruled by Fear
has a very, very high-pitched voice.
Like helium high.
Child Ruled by Fear, can you try to
say hello to me in that kind of voice?

> *DAVID works with the audience member reading for the child.*
> *They say "hello" back and forth, trying different voices.*
> *This establishes the child's vocal quality for the rest of the show.*
> *A high-pitched, soft voice.*

So, all of you sitting at the tables: that voice is
the voice of the Child Ruled by Fear.
Can we read the DEMONSTRATION one more time,
now that we know how the child sounds?

> *The two audience members read the DEMONSTRATION again.*
> *DAVID and the audience applaud.*

Perfect!

Before we start, there's one more thing everyone
in the room needs to be aware of.
At a few key moments, this story has a chorus.
Like a Greek chorus in a proper play.
The chorus lines will be read all together by
everyone in the room who'd like to join in:
those of you at the tables, and all of you on the risers.
The chorus lines will be projected on this big screen behind me,
and you'll know it's time to read chorus lines
when you hear this bell.

A bell rings.

So, for example:

A bell rings.

CHORUS
Hello
We are reading this line together
This line is projected on a screen

Yes it is!
The next time you hear that bell, you'll all know what to do.

All right, I think I've run out of things to explain to you.
Which means it's time for us to tell a story.
Tori, are we ready to start?

TORI says, "Places everybody. Places."

Nobody move: you're already there.
Okay, everybody.
This is the story of the Child Ruled by Fear

A bell rings.

CHORUS
This is the story of the Child Ruled by Fear

SCENE ONE

The Child Ruled by Fear came to be
In a landscape you and I can't see
A place with different gods and different matter
Different colours, thicker air, louder trees, different grass

And the Child Ruled by Fear wasn't exactly born
One day the Child Ruled by Fear just popped out of the ground

THE CHILD RULED BY FEAR
Waah! Waah! I've popped out of the ground!

Keening

THE CHILD RULED BY FEAR
Waaaaaaah!

Keening

THE CHILD RULED BY FEAR
Waaaaaaah!

Keening in a landscape with story but no history
Rhythm but no time
A place where a bell rings and all the people cry out

A bell rings.

CHORUS
We don't know what we are!
We don't know what we are!

A bell rings.

CHORUS
We don't know what we are!
We don't know what we are!

But there weren't any people yet
when the Child Ruled by Fear popped out of the ground
For the moment the Child Ruled by Fear was all alone
And the things in the world moved around at night
when the child wasn't looking
And whispered strange theories in mysterious voices

MYSTERIOUS VOICES
(whispering)
Strange theories strange theories strange theories

And the Child Ruled by Fear knew right away to be
spooked spooked spooked spooked spooked

THE CHILD RULED BY FEAR
Oh no

Said the Child Ruled by Fear

THE CHILD RULED BY FEAR
I am spooked spooked spooked spooked spooked

And for a while the landscape kept changing
The minor gods clicked their heels and the seas shook and splashed
Large granite broke up into smaller granite
Hot lava did something

THE CHILD RULED BY FEAR
Oh no oh no oh no

Said the Child Ruled by Fear

THE CHILD RULED BY FEAR
This is no place for a Child Ruled by Fear

And so fresh out of the ground
The Child Ruled by Fear ran and ran and ran and ran and ran

THE CHILD RULED BY FEAR
From a bush!
From a worm!
From a leaf!
From an ooze!

But you can't run away from the world

THE CHILD RULED BY FEAR
To the top of a hill!
To a rock by the sea!
To the shade of a tree!
Deep down in a hole!

But you can't run away from the world

Once the child spun around like a top
Around and around and around and around
And then puked all over an anthill
All over the little ants

THE CHILD RULED BY FEAR
I'm sorry I got you all pukey, you ants!
I'm trying to get away from the world!

THE PUKEY ANTS
You're crazy, you puker!
You can't get away from the world!

And the little pukey ants carried the Child Ruled by Fear to a river
And chucked the child in
And the river carried the child far far away

> **THE CHILD RULED BY FEAR**
> Oh no!
> The river carried me far far away!
> But I'm still in the world! I'm still in the world!

> **THE PUKEY ANTS**
> You're crazy, you puker!
> You can't get away from the world!

This went on and on
Until one day
The Child Ruled by Fear made a momentous discovery

> **THE CHILD RULED BY FEAR**
> Oh! Oh! Oh! Look!

> *Video: a close-up of* DAVID's *eye blinking.*

You can close your eyes, learned the Child Ruled by Fear
You have wipers for your tears and curtains for the sights
Built right into your fearful little head

> **THE CHILD RULED BY FEAR**
> Ta-dah!

And the Child Ruled by Fear was overjoyed with this new miracle

> **THE CHILD RULED BY FEAR**
> Wonderful!
> Wonderful!
> If I just shut these little curtains,
> I can fly over landscapes nothing like my own!

I soar and soar,
Carving shapes in the clouds as I go!
And then,
When I open these soft little curtains,
Then I can really see!

And the Child Ruled by Fear spent the days like this:
Content and alone
Just closing his eyes
Letting the world take his mind wherever it may

THE CHILD RULED BY FEAR
I'm standing by a small tree next to a small lake
on a big cliff under a big sky
I feel like the tree is just like me
I say hi, it says hi
Hi
Hi
Tree made of fear
Leaves made of fear
I'm standing in the wind
I'm swaying in the wind
There's light shining through me
It's gold
Chirp chirp in the distance
Chirp
Chirp
A tree
Breeze
Light
And slowly, slowly
I come apart
I blur and blur
I fade away

Breeze
Light
I dissolve
I fade away

SCENE TWO

Yes indeed, yes indeed
The Child Ruled by Fear had it all figured out
Shutting little curtains
Dissolving into light

And the Child Ruled by Fear looked up at
the minor gods, and proclaimed:

> **THE CHILD RULED BY FEAR**
> Aha, minor gods!
> You who watch over me and my landscape!
> You see how I've found my way!
> You see how good, how safe, how nice I feel!

> **THE MINOR GODS**
> Hmmmmm . . .

Said the minor gods

> **THE CHILD RULED BY FEAR**
> Minor gods! Minor gods!
> Look, I've found permanence!
> Peace! Light!

> **THE MINOR GODS**
> Hmmmmm . . .

Said the minor gods
And they giggled

THE MINOR GODS
Snrk

THE CHILD RULED BY FEAR
What?
What?

THE MINOR GODS
HMMMMMMM

Said the minor gods again
And they giggled more

THE MINOR GODS
Snrksnrksnrk
Tee hee
Heeheeheehee

THE CHILD RULED BY FEAR
Well what?!
You're just jealous, that's all

THE MINOR GODS
Haha
Haha
Hahahahahaha
HAHAHAHAHAHAHAH
HAHAHAHAHAHAHAHAHAHAHAHAHAHAHAHAHA HA HA HA!!!

THE CHILD RULED BY FEAR
Whatever!

Thought the Child Ruled by Fear

THE CHILD RULED BY FEAR
Big fat whatever!

But inside, the Child Ruled by Fear felt that old fear
Because the child heard something in that minor god laughter
Something like

THE MINOR GODS
Oh Child Ruled by Fear
You don't know the half of it
You can't be alone forever, Child Ruled by Fear
There's more to it than that
You're not ready, Child Ruled by Fear
You're not ready
You're only a child

And it was true, too
What the Child Ruled by Fear heard
in the laughter from the minor gods
It was there because the child knew it was true
And it rattled around in his brain for a long, long time
And the Child Ruled by Fear lived, and lived, and lived

One day a dust storm kicked up

A (sound and video) dust storm kicks up.

And the ground began to shake and churn

Shaking and churning.

And stars fell from the sky into the sea

A bell rings.

CHORUS
Weeeeeeeeeeeeee!

Creating great clouds of steam

A bell rings.

CHORUS
Tsssssssssssssssss

More stars fell from the sky into the sea

A bell rings.

CHORUS
Weeeeeeeeeeeeee!

Creating even greater clouds of steam

A bell rings.

CHORUS
Tsssssssssssssssss

And slowly
From all the shaking and churning and wind and sand and steam
A figure appeared

FLOOD
HELLO
I HAVE APPEARED

The figure towered over the Child Ruled by Fear
The Child Ruled by Fear looked up in awe

THE CHILD RULED BY FEAR
Wow

And thunder split the sky
And the howling trees howled
And the figure bellowed

FLOOD
MY NAME IS FLOOD
I AM HERE NOW
THIS IS MY ICE CREAM
YUM
YUM
YUM
I AM HERE I AM HERE
MY NAME IS FLOOD
HELLO

The Child Ruled by Fear just stared
Paralyzed by fear

FLOOD
WELL?
WELL?
AREN'T YOU GOING TO ASK ME FOR A LICK?

The Child Ruled by Fear just stared
Paralyzed by fear

FLOOD
ASK ME FOR A LICK OF MY ICE CREAM, CHILD

THE CHILD RULED BY FEAR
Oh um haha sure
Can I um
Can I have a lick of your ice cream child

FLOOD
HAHA! HAHA!
I LIKE YOU, CHILD RULED BY FEAR
YOU MAKE ME LAUGH, AND THAT'S GOOD!
GOOD, GOOD STUFF!
HAHA! HAHA!

THE CHILD RULED BY FEAR
Haha
Haha

FLOOD
LET'S BE FRIENDS, CHILD RULED BY FEAR
I'M HERE FOR FRIENDS!
I MAKE THEM EASILY AND GRACEFULLY!
MY NAME IS FLOOD AND I PUT PEOPLE AT EASE!
MY NATURE IS WINNING! MY MIND IS CLEAN!
HAVE A LICK HAVE A LICK OF MY BIG ICE CREAM!

And Flood moved to hand the Child Ruled by Fear
a big wet ice cream cone
Cold
And wet
And huge
The Child Ruled by Fear had never seen such a thing
And the child was afraid
And also the ice cream was really very big
And the Child Ruled by Fear was really very small
And so the ice cream fell on the ground

Video: the ice cream falls on the ground.

FLOOD
AAAAAAAAH
CHILD RULED BY FEAR
WHY ARE YOU LIKE THIS
YOU RUIN EVERYTHING FOR EVERYBODY
WHY CAN'T YOU JUST ENJOY SOMETHING FOR ONCE
YOUR ENERGY IS SO HARD TO BE AROUND
I'M JUST TRYING TO FIND A WAY TO LIVE MY LIFE
AND IT'S HARD ENOUGH AS IT IS, CHILD RULED BY FEAR
YOU'LL PAY FOR THIS, YOU'LL PAY FOR THIS, YOU'LL ALL PAY FOR THIS

THE CHILD RULED BY FEAR
But look
It's okay
I scooped 'er up
I scooped 'er right up

FLOOD
IT'S NOT GOING TO TASTE THE SAME
IT'S NOT GOING TO TASTE THE SAME
IT'S NOT GOING TO TASTE THE SAME
AAAAAAAAAAAAAAAAAAAAH!!!!!!!!!!!!!!

A (sound and video) snowstorm.

And the dust storm became a snowstorm
And Flood came apart and fell to pieces on the frozen ground

The storm continues, more quietly.

And when it was all over
The Child Ruled by Fear took a different look with
different eyes at the imaginary landscape
And saw that all the things looked different
Like all the things were scolding the child
Like all the things had aged

THE CHILD RULED BY FEAR
Hello?

But the things turned away

THE CHILD RULED BY FEAR
Hello??

But the things turned away

And this was the day that the Child Ruled by Fear
Learned to be afraid
Of the Child Ruled by Fear

THE CHILD RULED BY FEAR
Because what if I screw it up?
Am I bad?
Because what if I screw it up again?
Am I bad?
Because what if I screw it all up?
Am I bad? Am I bad? Am I bad?

The storm passes.

SCENE THREE

Things changed after the child met Flood
After Flood came the people
Many many many people
And the people built a city around the Child Ruled by Fear

> *DAVID produces a cardboard city from under his table.*
> *He places the CHILD RULED BY FEAR figurine in the city.*
> *A camera turns on, projecting live video of the child*
> *standing amongst the buildings.*
> *Then, every window in the city lights up from the inside.*
> *The child is standing in a glowing city at night.*

And the Child Ruled by Fear found a little apartment
On the second floor of a little building with some little stairs
And the Child Ruled by Fear got really into plants
And grinding dry-roasted beans for steeping in hot water

At nights when the weather got cool
The Child Ruled by Fear got into the habit of walking around
And the child would walk by many different people

And the people would say things like this

> *A bell rings.*

CHORUS

We are real

I know we are real

There's rain on my skin I can feel it

Everyone else seems so productive

Today I bought an air plant

That's a plant that grows with no dirt

I put it in a dish

Stop emailing my wife!

I'm aware I live near many other people

But I don't know any of their names

I'm aware I shouldn't smell these markers

And yet I keep smelling all these markers

A bird is a bird and also a miracle

We are real

We live lives

We have various concerns

We have loud beliefs and other quiet beliefs

We're not sure if it's good that we feel this way

We have so many things we don't know how to say

A short pause.

So that was how the city sounded
On a normal day

And the Child Ruled by Fear wandered to and fro, here and there
Looking and listening and trying to engage

And some days the Child Ruled by Fear felt very good
And found the city very beautiful
And other days the Child Ruled by Fear felt very bad
And became a little unstable
Difficult to be near

It was like the child was hearing hostile voices from hostile people
His voice but not his voice
Building pressure in his mind

And one day
The Child Ruled by Fear cracked open
And all the voices in his mind spilled out
all over a crowded city street

A bell rings.

CHORUS

Oh no

I can't live here

I shouldn't be here

I shouldn't be anywhere at all

I can't sleep

I can't eat

I can't take the heat

I can't take the rain

I can't take the constant scrutiny

I don't know what I believe

I don't know who I believe in

I don't know how to find out

I'm trying to find hope and I can't!

Hope keeps us going but should we keep going?

Do we just keep going and going and going?

I don't know how to be truthful!

I'm doing so many things so horribly horribly wrong!

A long pause.

SCENE FOUR

The song "Hellhole Ratrace" by the band Girls plays.

My name is David.
I have two email addresses.
They are davidfrederickwalker@gmail.com
and davidgagnonwalker@gmail.com,
which are two versions of my full name.
Please email me.
I'm very lonely.

I grew up straddling this country.
I'm kind of from Alberta and I'm kind of from Québec.
I have seen two devastating floods in my life.
One in 2013 in Calgary, Alberta,
and one in 1996 in Chicoutimi, Québec.

I live in Toronto but I don't really live in Toronto.
I don't think I really live anywhere.
I think I really live inside my own head.
My own head rarely feels much like home these days either.
These days nowhere feels quite right.

When I can't sleep I picture myself flying over imaginary landscapes.
These landscapes are full of strange colours and curves.

I hadn't heard this song in about five years until recently.

It's one of my favourite songs.
It's by Christopher Owens.
It's pretty good.

A long pause to listen to the song.

Christopher Owens grew up in a cult,
but he lives now in New York City and works in a coffee shop.
I pretty much assume I'm going to end up working
in a coffee shop again sometime soon.
What's so wrong with working in a coffee shop?
But it bothers me to think about.
I really do think I'm above it all.

I really do think I'm basically kind.
I've spent a lot of time saying very mean things
about people who I know are trying very hard.

Everyone I love most has pretty regular contact with depression.
I have pretty regular contact with depression.

When I was four, I pushed my little brother down some stairs,
and he had to get stitches,
and my aunt took me for ice cream at Baskin Robbins.
That same year I went to a petting zoo
and I was too scared to touch the cow.

I know I've scared people sometimes and that makes me feel so sad.

Sometimes when I have a phone call to make
I get so nervous I just start crying.

I'm always so nervous.

The world is so big and there's so much to see.

I really like being outside.
I don't feel at home anywhere.
I never feel very healthy.
I never feel very clean.

A long pause to listen to the song.

Anyway

SCENE FIVE

Live video of the cardboard city.
The CHILD RULED BY FEAR is lying down in the street.
· This sequence is a little object theatre show, with
live video, starring the child figurine.

It was wintertime
Dusk
And a wet snow had begun to fall

And a crowd had gathered around the Child Ruled by Fear
Who by now was just cowering in the street
after that fearful little outburst
And a tall figure with stooped shoulders and a long flowing coat
slowly approached the Child Ruled by Fear

The TALL FIGURE and her family are all made of
paper-towel rolls cut to various heights.
They all have googly eyes.

And the tall figure peeled off the long coat
And draped it over the Child Ruled by Fear
And said

THE TALL FIGURE
Come, friend
You seem like you could use some time in a warmly lit room
It's holiday time
There's family where I'm going
No one should spend holiday time alone

And the Child Ruled by Fear fell asleep in the tall figure's arms

> *DAVID places a living room backdrop in front of the city.*
> *On the live video, the CHILD RULED BY FEAR and the*
> *tall family are now in a cozy living room.*

When the child woke up
He was huddled in a ball in the middle of the floor
In a warmly lit room made of wood and stone

He watched the snow blowing around outside through the window
City people shuffled from their city jobs
to their city stores to their city homes

And a tall family huddled around the child
in a careful protective arch
Patient and curious and benign

The tall figure from the street had three tall children
A tall tall child

THE TALL TALL CHILD
Hello

A medium tall child

THE MEDIUM TALL CHILD
Hello

And a small tall child

THE SMALL TALL CHILD
Hello

The tall figure and the tall children stood
around the Child Ruled by Fear

All holding their hands together in front of themselves
Like this, as if in prayer
And eventually the tallest tall child said

THE TALL TALL CHILD
Is this small one well?

And the medium tall child said

THE MEDIUM TALL CHILD
To be so afraid in holiday time, this small one can't be well!

And the smallest tall child stooped all the way down
to the Child Ruled by Fear
And put a small face right next to the Child Ruled by Fear's
And said, quite simply

THE SMALL TALL CHILD
Hello

And the Child Ruled by Fear managed to turn his head
And managed a little smile

THE SMALL TALL CHILD
Hooray!
You see?
Anyone can be well in holiday time

THE MEDIUM TALL CHILD
We have to tell him the holiday tale!

THE TALL TALL CHILD
Oh yes the holiday tale! Please oh please! The holiday tale!

THE TALL FIGURE
Well, children

Said the tall elegant figure

THE TALL FIGURE
It is a fine night for a holiday tale

THE THREE CHILDREN
Hoooooray!

THE SMALL TALL CHILD
Can I be the voice in the moon?

THE TALL FIGURE
Of course, little one
You're always the voice in the moon

And huddled there in a ball on the floor of a warmly lit room
The Child Ruled by Fear heard the holiday tale
of Papa Tom and Little Dave

The live video dissolves to a pre-recorded object theatre movie.
Stop-motion animation.
A pageant put on by the three tall children, in
costumes, with a mountain backdrop.

DAVID turns to look at the screen.
He voices all the characters in the movie, speaking into the microphone.

Intro music to the movie:
an instrumental verse of "In the Bleak Midwinter."

Snow is falling in the movie.
PAPA TOM is watching the snow.
LITTLE DAVE enters.

LITTLE DAVE
Papa Tom! Papa Tom!

PAPA TOM
What is it, Little Dave?

LITTLE DAVE
Look, Papa Tom!
It's snowing!

PAPA TOM
So it is, Little Dave

LITTLE DAVE
You promised, Papa Tom
You promised
You said if I was a good boy all year
Then when the first snow came to Tom Tom Mountain
You'd tell me the story of Papa Tom and Little Dave

PAPA TOM
So I did, Little Dave

LITTLE DAVE
A Papa Tom should always keep his promise

PAPA TOM
So he should, Little Dave
Okay, Little Dave
I'll tell you, Little Dave
I'll tell you the story of Papa Tom and Little Dave

LITTLE DAVE
Oh yay, Papa Tom! Oh yay!

Flashback. The video becomes black and white. PAPA TOM *narrates.*

PAPA TOM
The story starts on a snowy night long ago
Papa Tom was sitting alone on Tom Tom Mountain
Papa Tom was all alone, Little Dave
There used to be all kinds of people on Tom Tom Mountain
But then there were the disasters
And Papa Tom was all alone
And Papa Tom looked up at the snow and the stars in the sky
And said
Oh, oh
Will Papa Tom always be alone?
And then, Little Dave
Papa Tom heard a voice
A voice that whispered on the wind
And Papa Tom saw a light
A glowing light from the moon up above
And the voice was coming from the moon up above!
And the voice spoke to Papa Tom!

The moon appears.
This is the SMALL TALL CHILD *in a moon costume,*
hanging from a rope above PAPA TOM.

THE VOICE IN THE MOON
Papa Tom
Papa Tom
Here, for you, Papa Tom
A Little Dave
A little baby
A little rock baby
A little baby Little Dave

PAPA TOM
And floating down from the light of the moon
Was a little rock baby!
A little baby Little Dave!

A rock with googly eyes floats down from overhead.

ROCK BABY LITTLE DAVE
Waaaaa! Waaaaa!

PAPA TOM
And the voice in the moon spoke again

THE VOICE IN THE MOON
Papa Tom
We've given you a Little Dave
A Little Dave of your very own
But this Little Dave has a price, Papa Tom
You'll raise this Little Dave to be good
And this Little Dave will take your place
And you'll say goodbye to your Little Dave
And you will come to us
You'll follow the light of the moon
And be our Papa Tom
When the Little Dave is ready
When it's the first snow of the year
You will tell the story of Papa Tom and Little Dave
And you'll come to the moon
And Papa Tom and Little Dave
Will have to say goodbye

PAPA TOM
Oh no
Oh no oh no oh no oh no

Flash to the present. The video goes back to colour.

PAPA TOM
That's the story, Little Dave
Do you understand, Little Dave?

LITTLE DAVE
No, Papa Tom!
You can't go, Papa Tom!
I'm not ready, Papa Tom!

PAPA TOM
Look, Little Dave
The light of the moon

LITTLE DAVE
Oh no!

PAPA TOM
I'm going, Little Dave
Be good, Little Dave
I love you, Little Dave

LITTLE DAVE
I love you, Papa Tom

PAPA TOM
I love you, Little Dave
I'm going, Little Dave
Goodbye, Little Dave
Goodbye

LITTLE DAVE
Papa Tom!
Oh, Papa Tom
Oh, night sky
Oh, stars
Oh, pretty, pretty snow

Closing music to the movie:
an instrumental verse of "In the Bleak Midwinter."
The movie ends.

Back to live video of the objects on the table.

And by the end of the holiday tale
The Child Ruled by Fear had uncurled
from his little ball on the ground
And the Child Ruled by Fear lay there
Looking up at the tasteful exposed filament bulb in the family light
Quietly repeating

THE CHILD RULED BY FEAR
I'm all alone
I'm all alone
I'm all alone
I'm all alone
I'm all alone

And after a few minutes of this, the tall tall child said

THE TALL TALL CHILD
I'm confused
The child's not alone
We're all right here

THE TALL FIGURE
Shhhh

Smiled the tall figure from the street

THE TALL FIGURE
You're not wrong
But
That's just how some people are

And the Child Ruled by Fear quivered a little

THE TALL FIGURE
Say, small fearful one
How would you like to stay with us for a while?

And the Child Ruled by Fear did stay for a while
with these tall figures
And holiday time stretched on and on
And the wet snow blew and blew
It blew so you couldn't see your hand in front of your own face
And so nobody went outside for a very long time

Pause.

And one day the Child Ruled by Fear
thanked his tall surrogate family

THE CHILD RULED BY FEAR
Thank you for all your help
But of course, I mustn't stay forever
I'm ready to face the world

THE TALL FIGURE
Of course, Child Ruled by Fear
That's what people in the world are for, isn't it?
Helping you with your little fear

And they all bowed a tall, sarcastic bow

And they never saw the Child Ruled by Fear again

DAVID puts the paper-towel-roll family back under his table.

SCENE SIX

The Child Ruled by Fear stepped out into the street
And the world whirred and buzzed all around his fearful head

THE CHILD RULED BY FEAR
Oh boy
I really live here

Said the Child Ruled by Fear

THE CHILD RULED BY FEAR
Maybe this might be all right
Maybe everything is going to be okay

Which of course
Was a cursed thing to say
Drum roll please

> DAVID *and the audience do a drum roll on their tables and laps.*
> *The drum roll on* DAVID's *table causes the live video image of the city*
> *to shake like an earthquake.*

> *Live video out.*

And just as the Child Ruled by Fear uttered this foolish curse
The streets began to shake
Night birds shrieked in the middle of day
Cyclists flew by wailing "Heartless! Heartless! Holy! Fear!"

> *A bell rings.*

CHORUS
Heartless! Heartless! Holy! Fear!
Heartless! Heartless! Holy! Fear!

And the air grew damp and cold
And a voice came from everywhere at once

FLOOD
I TOLD YOU, CHILD RULED BY FEAR
I TOLD YOU YOU'D PAY FOR THIS
MY NAME IS FLOOD
I CAME HERE TO MAKE FRIENDS AND YOU IGNORED MY NEED
NOW THIS IS HAPPENING
REMEMBER MY NAME
REMEMBER MY NAAAAAAAAAAAAME

A bell rings.

CHORUS
FLOOD!
FLOOD!
FLOOD!
FLOOD!
FLOOD!
FLOOD!
FLOOD!
FLOOD!
FLOOOOOOOOOOOD!

A great, terrible flood.

Video: news footage of the Chicoutimi 1996 and Calgary 2013 floods.
Rushing water destroying a neighbourhood in Chicoutimi.
All of downtown Calgary under several feet
of water, seen from overhead.

A loud sound of rushing water.

DAVID puts the cardboard city back under the table.
He turns around and watches the video for a long while.

He turns back to face the audience.

And so everything changed in a great terrible wave
A tall family washed away
A wise grandma washed away
Many domesticated animals washed away
And the Child Ruled by Fear
Who had no inner density
Spongy, like bird bones
Floated on the torrent
Gaping at its awful beauty
Passive as the Child Ruled by Fear always was
And it was almost peaceful
Almost a relief
And the Child Ruled by Fear drifted off to sleep

Nighttime, stars.

And the minor gods looked down

THE MINOR GODS
Hehehehe
Hahahaha
Sweet sad Child Ruled by Fear
You've been through a lot
We've enjoyed your long time in this invisible land
It's time to start looking for an ending
It's time we introduce you to our friend

SCENE SEVEN

The sea began to churn and foam
And a whirlpool formed

And from the centre of the whirlpool
emerged something like a hand
Which scooped up the Child Ruled by Fear
And gathered him up out of the water
And held him there
Suspended between the glittering surface of the sea
and the glittering surface of the night sky

This was a major god
A powerful ancient lever on the world
And this was the night that the Child Ruled by Fear met Fear

FEAR is played by the bucket from the top of the show, voiced by DAVID.
DAVID puts it on his head and speaks softly into the mic.
His voice is pitch-shifted to be very low.
He is filmed by a live video camera.
The video shot contains the projection screen,
creating a video feedback loop.
Infinite faces on infinite buckets.

FEAR
Hi
Nice to see you

                        THE CHILD RULED BY FEAR
                             It's weird
                          I feel so calm

Pause.

THE CHILD RULED BY FEAR
I know who you are
There's no way I should feel calm
I never feel this calm
How am I so calm?

FEAR
Why shouldn't you be?

THE CHILD RULED BY FEAR
Well because you
You're

FEAR
Fear

THE CHILD RULED BY FEAR
Yeah

FEAR
And you
Are the Child Ruled by Fear

THE CHILD RULED BY FEAR
Yeah

FEAR
So

THE CHILD RULED BY FEAR
So?

FEAR
Think about it
If I'm always with you
And I *am* always with you
And if you're always fighting with me
And you *are* always fighting with me
Of course you're going to feel unwell

THE CHILD RULED BY FEAR
So you just follow me around?
All the time?

FEAR
You could say that
Something like that

THE CHILD RULED BY FEAR
Why?

FEAR
The idea is to help you
So you move when you need to move

Pause.

THE CHILD RULED BY FEAR
Okay but then
Why am I always like
It's like
Like I'm trying to breathe and I can't
It's like I'm trying to breathe and I can't
Like every thought in my head flicks a switch in my head
to light up another thought in my head
And they're all terrible
They're all really really bad

Why am I just meeting you now
if you've been here this whole time?

Pause.

FEAR
But you are breathing

THE CHILD RULED BY FEAR
Yeah but—

FEAR
You are
. . .
. . .
Here's what's going to happen
There's going to be a whole period that feels like an ending
What looks like it's happening really will be happening
There will be cause for anger and grief and yearning and guilt
Most of it will feel insurmountable and that feeling will be accurate
There will once have been a thing called coral
There will once have been a thing called flight
You'll think you're alone but you won't be alone
And you'll find that the world made you buoyant
And you'll float right up over these depths
This was drawn in ancient blueprints
long before you came from the ground
This was all preventable but it wasn't meant to be prevented
You'll build pontoons and sails and lifeboats and nets
and new cities fit for life without land
You'll find comfort in others just like you
You'll bear guilt together
You'll all convalesce
You'll float and you'll float and you'll breathe and you'll breathe

A long pause.

THE CHILD RULED BY FEAR
There's really no other way to do this?
There's really no other way to live?

FEAR
Child Ruled by Fear
The borders of your mind are real borders
This is how everything lives

THE CHILD RULED BY FEAR
Um

DAVID takes the bucket off his head and puts the mic down.
Video out.

And just as gently as what goes up went up
What goes down of course went down
And something like a hand lowered the child
back down to the surface of the water
And Fear faded back into the stars

And the night breeze did its soft little thing
And the Child Ruled by Fear bobbed along

SCENE EIGHT

Eventually the sun rose on this watery imaginary world

And the Child Ruled by Fear opened his eyes

Video: a close-up of DAVID'S *eye opening.*

THE CHILD RULED BY FEAR
Oh my
I've had an amazing terrible dream

And the Child Ruled by Fear raised his small head
and looked around

Video: the CHILD RULED BY FEAR *floating in water.*

And he saw that the water really was water
And he saw that the water was all there was
And he found that he was floating
And he paused for a very long time

Pause for a very long time.

There weren't any more people
The child seemed to be floating alone

But when he closed his eyes he could hear all the people still

A bell rings.

CHORUS

I remember swimming in the river

I remember wondering whether it was clean

I remember making snow angels at age nine
with a girl named Danielle

I remember watching a lot of news

I remember glass windows and glass doors

I remember going whale-watching and never seeing a single whale

I remember running

I remember bars

I remember feeling sorry for myself

I remember trying to apologize

I remember lying and thinking no one would know I was lying

I remember sleeping in the back seat of a van
with my orange cowboy blanket

I remember climbing a mountain
and feeling very big
and feeling very small

A long pause.

And as I hear these voices inside my mind
I find myself suddenly feeling very hot

THE CHILD RULED BY FEAR
Oh . . . wow . . . oh . . . my

The heat is coming from inside my chest
And it builds up like a pressure
And it glows from within a deep dark red
I have nowhere to go and nothing to do

THE CHILD RULED BY FEAR
I have nowhere to go and nothing to do
And so I just have to feel this feeling
I burn and crackle and throb
I feel something stirring deep in the centre of my chest
Something craning its neck
and snapping its beak
and rustling its wings

And this is when I learn
That in the centre of my chest there lives an idea
An idea something put there long ago

And that idea is an albatross
And that albatross is trapped there
And its name is salvation
And it is made of glass

THE CHILD RULED BY FEAR
And at that moment
The great bird rises out of my chest
And stretches out its great glass wings
And looks around wearily
And gracefully flies away

There's something indescribable in the eyes of animals
Their eyes, and their bearing, and their silence

Silence.

And in the space where once was trapped salvation
A new heavy feeling rushes in
And I stop floating
And slowly begin to sink

THE CHILD RULED BY FEAR
The water is light blue
And then a darker blue
And then a darker blue
The light from above gets further and further away

And I settle at the bottom of the ocean
And I keep waiting for a moment that feels like an ending
And to my quiet surprise that moment never comes

I don't have to float
I don't have to breathe
I don't have to understand
It doesn't have to be okay

THE CHILD RULED BY FEAR
I don't have to float
I don't have to breathe
I don't have to understand
It doesn't have to be okay

A few creatures are already down here
And many others join in time
And things keep happening
Although nothing is saved

And so looking very little like it did before
The imaginary landscape keeps changing
And invisible gatherings form

A bell rings.

CHORUS
And that was the story of the Child Ruled by Fear

And that was the story of the Child Ruled by Fear

EPILOGUE

Gradual darkness.
Only DAVID's table remains lit.

There are two times in my recent life I felt the world was magic.

The first I was on a beach.
I had just arrived that night to meet my
partner's family on vacation in Hawaii.
At first I didn't want to go because I'm an idiot, but I went.
It was pretty late at night,
and we walked down to the beach.
There wasn't anyone else there.
And we sat on the sand on a towel
and looked up at the stars.
We could see many, many stars.
And we noticed some of them were flying across the sky.

Weeeeeeeeeeeeee!

There was a meteor shower that night.
I'd heard about it, but I'd forgotten.
Then I watched it on a beach.

And after some time watching the flickering lights
drawing fine lines in the night sky,
we noticed something else.
We noticed other lights,
white-blue, almost the same colour as the stars,
washing in from the dark ocean and onto the beach.

Hundreds of them, these mysterious blue lights
gently floating to shore,
as other mysterious blue lights traced gentle lines overhead.
We sat there for a very long time.

The next morning we went down to the same spot,
and the beach was littered with tiny dead squid.
The squid had transparent little bodies like a night light.
They must have been bioluminescent.
They washed up to the sand to die.

The second time was in the backyard of a rental house
in Edmonton, where I'm from.
We all called this place the mansion.
It was huge and a bunch of people lived there
and it wasn't really very well maintained.
Once late at night one of my friends who
lived there said hey, come out back.
I have to show you something.
You have to hear this.

So we went out to the backyard.
It was pretty dark, there weren't any lights back there.
The grass must have been a foot and a half tall.
The ground seemed weird underfoot, too soft almost, really wet.
It had rained a lot that summer, I didn't think much of it.
And so we got to the middle of the yard.
And my friend said okay,
listen to this.
And he stomped on the ground.
And I heard a sound unlike anything I'd ever heard before.

And he said you try.
And I stomped on the ground.
And I felt what I thought was the ground,
everything underfoot all around me,

scurry away from my feet in every direction.
The sound was sudden and slurpy and almost shockingly loud.

The thing was the grass was full of slugs.
A thick layer of slugs covering the entire surface of the backyard.
Probably several slugs thick.
There must have been thousands of them.

I think.
That's what my friend said, anyway.
It's hard to know for sure.
It was pitch black, and the grass was long,
and nobody I know lives there anymore.

Thank you all very much for joining me.
Thank you all very much for being here.

End of play.

ACKNOWLEDGEMENTS

Thanks to Christian Barry, Judy Wensel, Morgan Melenka, Patricia Vinluan, and Lauren Acheson for helping Tori and me make this idea real. This process felt how I always hoped a process could.

Thanks to everyone at 2b theatre company during my residency in 2019/20, particularly Anthony Black and Karen Gross, for the amazing year in Halifax and for helping nurture the seeds of this project.

Thanks to Marcus Youssef for crucial thoughts and encouragement early in the writing.

Thanks to the Canada Council for the Arts and the National Theatre School of Canada for financial support.

Thanks to the presenters who have invited us to share this work with your audiences in your cities, and to all the staff and volunteers who have made every presentation a joy.

Thanks to everyone who has listened to or helped tell this story.

Thanks to my teachers for helping me find this path.

Thanks to my friends for giving my life meaning.

Thanks to Mom, Dad, and Daniel for showing me what love looks like.

Most of all, thanks to Tori Morrison. I'm so grateful for the world we've made together, and for all the worlds inside that world.

David Gagnon Walker is a writer, performer, and translator born in Edmonton and based in Toronto. His work has been performed and developed in cities across Canada, and through residencies in Sweden, Finland, France, Australia, and the USA. His awards include the Playwrights Guild of Canada RBC Emerging Playwright Award for *The Big Ship*, first prize in the Wildfire National Playwriting Competition for *Pink Moon*, and the Playwrights' Workshop Montréal Cole Foundation Mentorship for Emerging Translators. Other plays include *Premium Content* (Major Matt Mason Collective/High Performance Rodeo), *The Last Children* (Curtain Razors), and the English translation of Gabrielle Chapdelaine's *The Retreat* (Imago Theatre). David is Artistic Producer of Strange Victory Performance, a collaboration with composer and video designer Tori Morrison, through which he has been touring experimental and interactive performance projects since 2020. He holds an M.A. in Performance Studies from the University of Toronto and is a graduate of the playwriting program at the National Theatre School of Canada.